ENVIRONMENTAL
ISSUES

PUBLISHING

By Emilie Dufresne

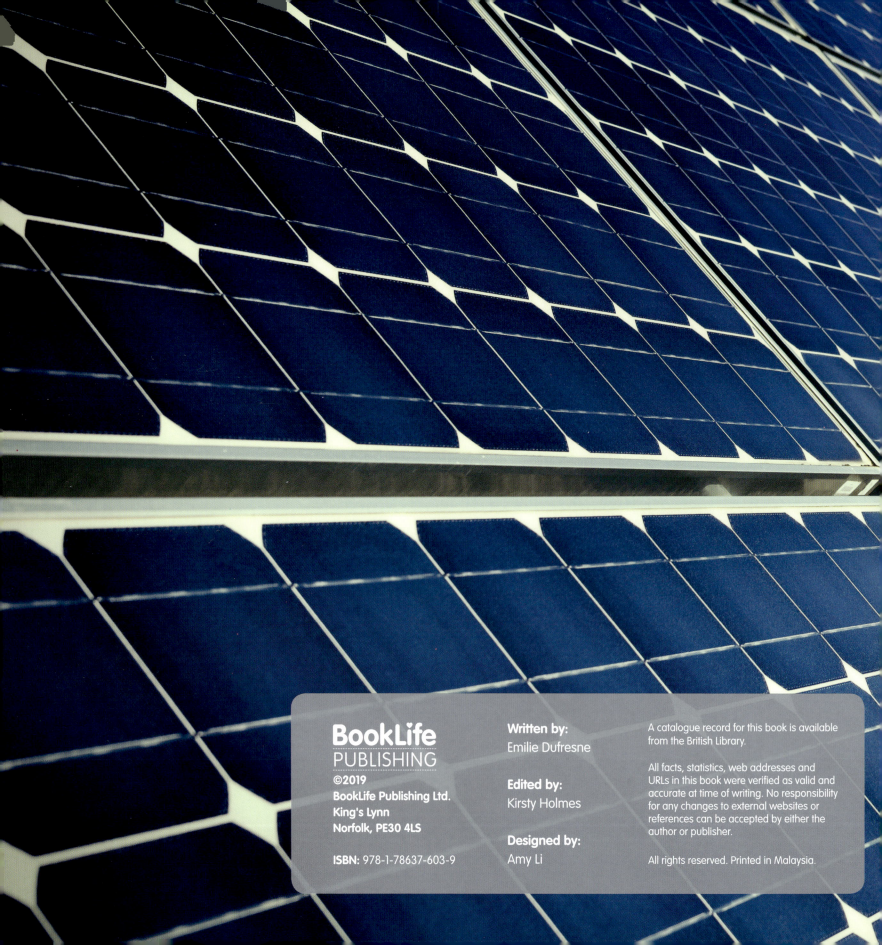

BookLife
PUBLISHING

©2019
BookLife Publishing Ltd.
King's Lynn
Norfolk, PE30 4LS

ISBN: 978-1-78637-603-9

Written by:
Emilie Dufresne

Edited by:
Kirsty Holmes

Designed by:
Amy Li

CONTENTS

Words that look like **this** can be found in the glossary on page 24.

RENEWABLE AND NON-RENEWABLE ENERGY

There are two different types of energy that are used to make power. These are renewable and non-renewable. Renewable energy is energy that we can keep making more of so that it doesn't run out.

THESE WIND TURBINES CREATE RENEWABLE ENERGY.

Non-renewable energy comes from materials that will eventually run out. Some non-renewable energy sources include coal and oil.

OIL RIG

WHY DO WE NEED RENEWABLE ENERGY?

We need renewable energy sources for two main reasons. The first reason is that, one day, non-renewable energy sources will run out.

WITHOUT RENEWABLE ENERGY SOURCES WE WOULD BE LEFT WITHOUT POWER AND HEAT.

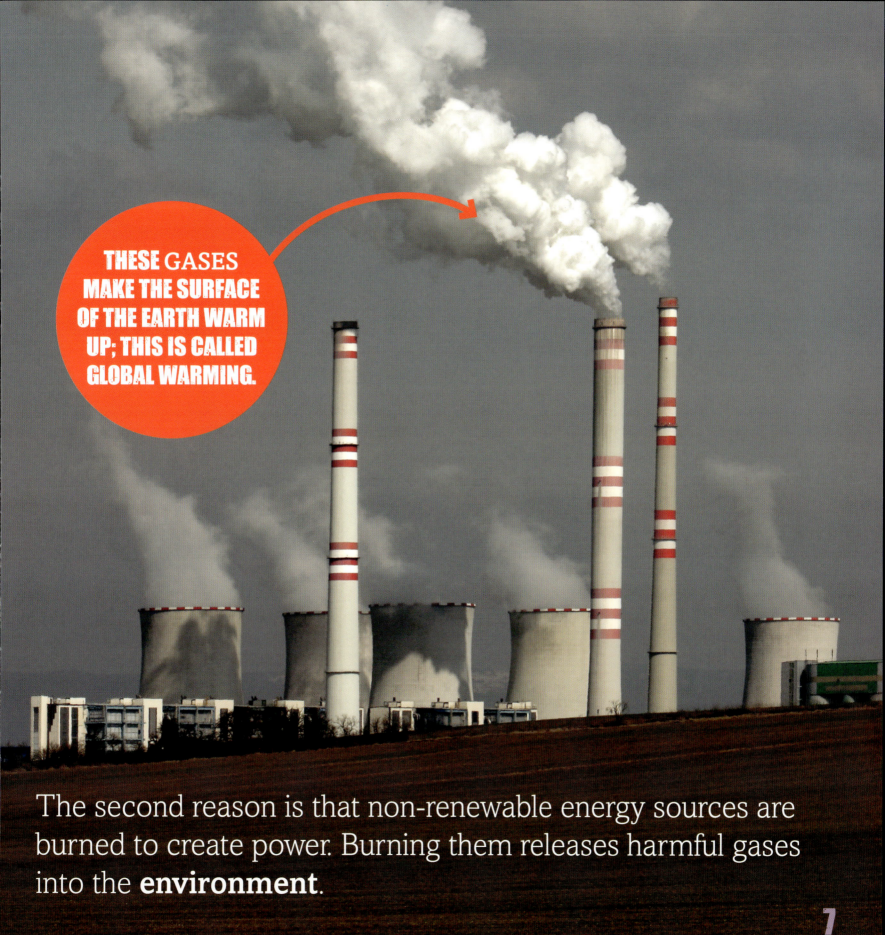

THESE GASES MAKE THE SURFACE OF THE EARTH WARM UP; THIS IS CALLED GLOBAL WARMING.

The second reason is that non-renewable energy sources are burned to create power. Burning them releases harmful gases into the **environment**.

TYPES OF RENEWABLE ENERGY

Renewable energy uses the world's natural resources to create energy. For example, heat and energy can be collected both from the Sun and from deep under the Earth's surface.

THIS HEAT CAN BE USED TO HEAT UP HOMES OR MAKE ELECTRICITY.

HYDROELECTRIC POWER PLANT

'HYDRO' MEANS WATER. THIS PLANT USES WATER TO CREATE ELECTRICITY.

The movement of wind and water can also be used to create energy. As water flows through rivers or wind flows through the sky, they can turn turbines which can **generate** energy.

SOLAR POWER

Solar panels can be put anywhere: on the roof of a house, in large fields, or even the sides of buildings. The panels contain special cells that capture energy from the Sun and turn it into heat and electricity.

If we could **harness** all of the energy we get from the Sun in one hour, it would be enough to power everything on Earth for a whole year.

WIND POWER

Wind turbines can either be used in a group, called a wind farm, or on their own for a single building. The wind spins the blades; this powers a generator which creates electricity.

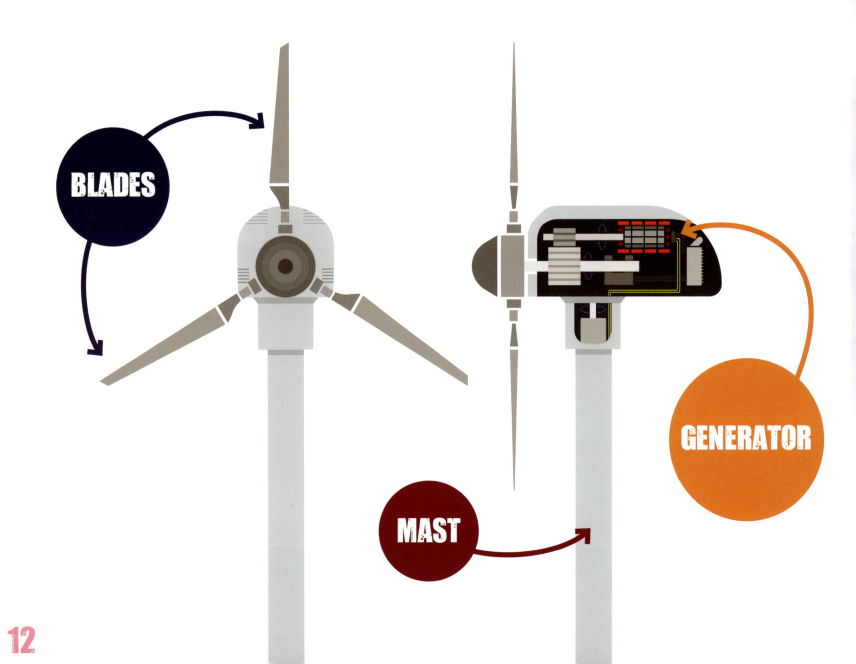

BLADES

MAST

GENERATOR

Wind turbines are getting bigger and taller. The bigger a wind turbine is, the more energy it can make. Today, most wind turbines are as tall as the Statue of Liberty.

HYDROPOWER

Hydropower uses the power created by moving water to create electricity. This can be done from rivers flowing downstream, water falling from dams, and the moving tides in the sea.

TIDAL ENERGY FARM

Hydropower is a very **efficient** source of renewable energy.
It can create power all day long and whenever it is needed,
rather than just creating power when it is windy or sunny.

GEOTHERMAL POWER

Geothermal energy is heat that we get from the Earth. The Earth contains heat from volcanic areas or areas with **geysers**.

'GEO' MEANS 'FROM THE EARTH' AND 'THERMAL' MEANS 'HEAT'.

GEOTHERMAL ENERGY PLANT, ICELAND

Geysers and volcanoes heat up rocks and water underground. Pipes can be placed near these hot areas underground. The pipes can send cold water to the warmer areas to heat up.

THE WATER IS WARMED UP AND BROUGHT BACK THROUGH THE PIPES TO HEAT HOMES.

PROBLEMS WITH RENEWABLE ENERGY

Hydroelectric dams can be seen as bad because they damage where fish live and **migrate**. The dams stop the fish swimming to the rivers they normally go to.

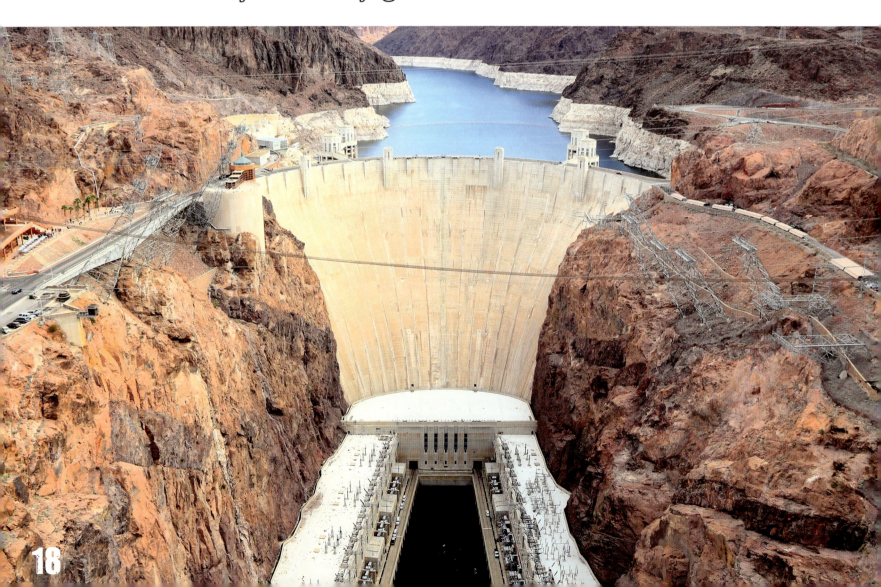

To generate lots of electricity from solar power, lots of solar panels are needed. Often these solar panels are built in large farms. Solar farms take up the space where lots of plants and animals could live.

RENEWABLE ENERGY FACTS

Some of the world's most powerful wind turbines have blades that are bigger than the London Eye. The blades are so powerful that just one spin could power a UK home for a whole day.

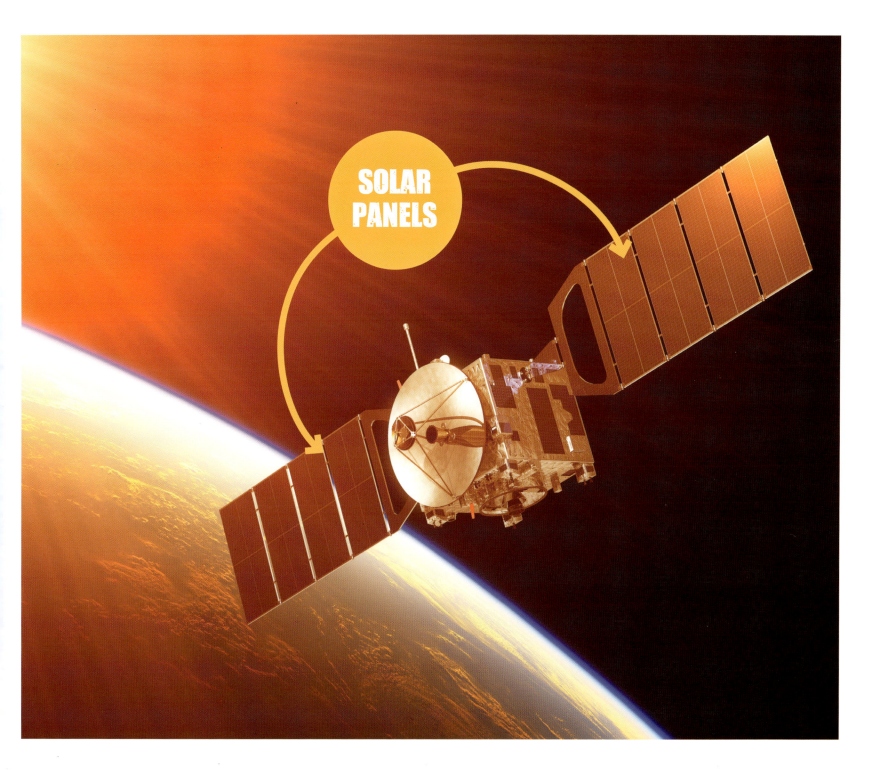

Lots of **satellites** in the Earth's orbit have solar panels on them. This means they will never run out of energy and can stay in space for many years.

HOW WE CAN HELP

There are lots of things people can do to use renewable energy. We can buy electric cars, or put solar panels on our houses.

YOU CAN ALWAYS ASK YOUR PARENTS IF THEY USE RENEWABLE ENERGY SOURCES.

GET PEDDLING

There are still things you can do to cut down on using non-renewable energy. If you can, walk or ride your bike to school instead of going in the car.

CUT DOWN ON WASTE

Always remember to recycle anything you can. Lots of harmful gases are released from rubbish.

GLOSSARY

efficient	getting the most out of something in the best way possible
environment	the natural world
gases	matter that is air-like and fills any space available
generate	to create or make
geysers	hot springs that shoot out steam and hot water
harness	to make use of
migrate	when animals move from one place to another based on changes in weather
satellites	machines in space that travel around planets, take photographs and collect and send information
turbines	machines that look similar to fans and are driven by air or water pushing against the blades, making them move

INDEX

Photocredits – Images are courtesy of Shutterstock.com. With thanks to Getty Images, Thinkstock Photo and iStockphoto.
Cover – ngoc tran, Tamara Kulinova, Boris15, 1 – ixpert, 2 – VioNet, 3 – OKAWA PHOTO, 4 – pavels, 5 – Wisit Tongma, 6 – Andrey_Popov, 7 – Kodda, 8 – Diyana Dimitrova, 9 – Maxim Burkovskiy, 10 – xieyuliang, 11 – Aphellon, 12 – Tatyana TVK, 13 – Diyana Dimitrova, 14 – Alex Mit, 15 – Capricorn Studio, 16 – Tony Craddock, 17 – N. Minton, 18 – Tupungato, 19 – Michael Dechev, 20 – iweta0077, 21 – 3Dsculptor, 22 – Air Images, 23 – KK Tan, Rawpixel.com.